JE SUIS CHARLIE

The Charlie Hebdo Newspaper Massacre

Patricia Crouch

CONTENTS

CHAPTER ONE

Famous Last Words

"There haven't been any attacks in France . . ."

Photo: The Place de république, Paris, France, in 2014[1]

The week of the January 7, 2015, attack on the small satirical newspaper *Charlie Hebdo*, a cartoon in the paper observed in its caption, "There haven't been any attacks in France." Presumably the line referred to the still-new year. Below the caption, a turbaned man depicted with a rifle strapped to his back replies, "Wait! We still have until the end of January to extend our wishes."

In France, as the BBC reports, it's traditional to "offer New Year's greetings until the end of January."

An ominous response appeared the morning of the attack, before the news broke, in the form of a cartoon tweeted from *Charlie Hebdo*'s account. It depicted Abu Bakr al-Baghdadi, a leader of the jihadist Islamic State, responding to a caption that said, "Best wishes. To you too, Al-Baghdadi." In reply, the figure says, "And especially good health."[2] Within hours, the macabre irony of the cartoon would be apparent to the world as the tragic events at *Charlie Hebdo* were made public.

The same morning that the tweeted comic was sent, the newspaper staff, according to *Charlie Hebdo* columnist Patrick Pelloux, was attending a "meeting discussing a conference on the fight against racism."[3] Two gunmen armed with assault rifles forced their way into the newspaper's Paris offices, where they shot and killed ten people, among them the paper's editorial director Stéphane Charbonnier and some of the weekly's most popular cartoonists. The assailants then made their escape with the aid of an accomplice. Two policemen were killed during the attack, and numerous other people were wounded.

Witnesses reported that during the assault, the gunmen shouted "Allah akbar" (Arabic for "God is great"), while an amateur video recorded their cries of, "We have avenged the Prophet Muhammad! We have killed Charlie Hebdo!"[4]

Charlie Hebdo columnist Zineb El Rhazoui, who was absent from the meeting, later recounted how Charbonnier had been in the habit of mocking "his Islamist critics by using 'Allah Akbar' as his sign-off on emails and text messages . . . One day, we had this conversation at the newspaper, for a laugh, 'Charb, stop yelling that—the day they come to bump you off, we won't know whether it's a joke!' And it happened. We knew, at *Charlie*, that humor had something very serious about it."[5]

French President François Hollande decried the attack as an act of "barbarism." In his words, it was an attack on "the expression of freedom" that is the "spirit of the republic."[6]

In the hours and days that followed, thousands would gather and march at Paris's Place de république to show solidarity with Charlie Hebdo and give voice to their support for the principles of free speech that the paper's surviving members championed brazenly on its home page following the massacre. This public outpouring for the financially strapped, small-circulation weekly—it usually prints less than 60,000 copies and "recently issued appeals on its website for financial support"—was decidedly disproportionate to the size of its readership, demonstrating that the attack had touched a collective nerve.[7]

Against the terrorists' cries that they had "killed Charlie Hebdo," the web site offered proof of life, shouting, "JE SUIS CHARLIE" ("I am Charlie"). Accompanying the declaration was an image of an upraised hand clenching a pen and a headline-sized version of the familiar phrase, "the pen is mightier than the sword." It read, "the pen is higher than barbarism."

Photo: The Place de république, Paris, France, January 11, 2015[8]

As the "preferred departure point for many left-wing demonstrations," the Place de république was the ideal site at which to hold a public vigil for freedom of the press. Inaugurated to celebrate the French Republic, its central visual sign is a statue of Marianne, "a symbol of the French state, [who] sits on a carved stone column that is decorated with allegories of liberté, égalité, and fraternité [liberty, equality, and fraternity]." In her right hand, Marianne clutches the symbol of peace, the olive branch, while in her left she holds "a tablet inscribed with the Rights of Man (les Droits de l'Homme)."[9] Standing on and around the statue in January 2015, demonstrators carried signs declaring, "Je Suis Charlie," showing their solidarity with the magazine and its fervent championing of free speech.

Photo: A memorial at the Place de république, Paris, France, January 8, 2015[10]

Around the world—including Dublin, Berlin, Moscow, Edinburgh, Rio de Janeiro, Amsterdam, Brussels, Madrid, Rome, and Madagascar, and at such sites as Union Square in New York and Trafalgar Square in London—similar vigils, often hosting thousands and sometimes as many as four million supporters, sprang up. Demonstrators carried the same "Je Suis Charlie" signs, or translated versions such as the English "I am Charlie."

In the media, and in the spectator's first-glance impressions, these enormous and prolific demonstrations visually embodied an unbroken international, if not universal, fraternity.

There were some, though, who could not help but ask the question of what exactly supporters were announcing about themselves when they carried signs identifying them as "Charlie."

It was not only placards declaring "Je Suis Charlie" that could be found among the demonstrators at these international vigils. A protester who attended a gathering at the French consulate on a bitterly cold night in Montreal, wearing a hood and with face bundled in a scarf, carried a handwritten sign declaring, "Et je blaspheme si je veux": "And I blaspheme if I want to."

Photo: At a vigil before the French embassy in Montreal, January 7 2015[11]

The sign's hand-written uniqueness marked it as offering a minority version of the exemplary, mass-printed "Je Suis Charlie" sign visible just in the background.

The photographer who captured the image of this bundled figure, Gerry Lauzon, entitled the work "Rien à foutre," or "Fuck." The caption gestures toward the sign's satirical play on the magazine's own historical claims to be offering satire protected under the laws of free speech. In revising the "Je Suis Charlie" slogan, the placard both cites those rights and makes visible the alternative interpretation that can—and has—been made of *Charlie Hebdo*'s work. Namely, that instead of offering thought-provoking, critical satire, it brazenly blasphemes the Islamic (and other) religions in a cavalier, immoral way.

The purpose of this book is to explore the narrative and counter-narrative of *Charlie Hedbo* embodied in the competing photographs just described—both the majority and the minority reports on the newspaper's history and its actions. If we consider the massacre within the full range of its contexts, we are required to interrogate the media's often simplistic representation of the 2015 attack as an expression of the "culture clash between religious extremism and the West's devotion to free expression," to use the words of one *New York Times* writer.[12]

To be clear, this book in no way offers a defense of the terrorist actions taken by Al-Qaida extremists against the staff of *Charlie Hebdo*. But it does invite the reader to consider alternate views of the magazine's satirical representations of Islam and its Prophet Muhammad and, in doing so, to move critically beyond an easy acceptance of the newspaper as a purely heroic champion of "free speech."

In short, it asks the question, what do we mean if we say of ourselves, "Je Suis Charlie"?

CHAPTER TWO

Charlie to Islam:

"A newspaper is not a weapon of war"

— Gerard Biard, editor-in-chief of Charlie Hebdo[13]

Outside Charlie Hebdo*'s Offices after the 2011 Fire-Bombing*[14]

The 2015 massacre was not the first act of terrorism perpetrated by Islamic extremists against the small, financially struggling *Charlie Hebdo*. Its offices were fire-bombed in 2011. The weekly has been repeatedly threatened over the years for its caricatures of the Prophet Muhammad and other subjects, and its web site was briefly shut down by a cyberattack in 2012. As one writer notes, "It was an obvious target and editor Stéphane Charbonnier and his staff were under full-time police protection."[15]

Charbonnier, who perished in the 2015 attack, repeatedly ignored pleas from the French government to use caution, once explaining, "It's perhaps a bit pompous, what I'm about to say, but I would rather die standing than to live on my knees."[16]

The newspaper's refusal to bow to the pressures of Islamic fundamentalists was perhaps nowhere more evident than in its decision to reprint the twelve now-infamous Danish cartoons from 2005 depicting the Prophet Muhammad and other Islamic subjects. The cartoons first appeared in *Jyllands-Posten* and were reprinted in *Charlie Hebdo* in February 2006, sparking protests in France and riots in the Middle East.

A February 11, 2006, protest in Paris of Charlie Hebdo's publication of the Danish cartoons[17]

Two of the cartoons were particularly inflammatory. In the first, Muhammad was represented wearing a turban with a bomb inside it, implying that he was orchestrating Islamic terrorist attacks. The other depicted the prophet "welcoming a line of suicide bombers to heaven with the words 'Stop, stop, we have run out of virgins!'"[18]

Besides reprinting the Danish illustrations, *Charlie Hebdo* created an original cover illustration for the issue. Entitled "Muhammad and the Fundamentalists," the cartoon depicted Muhammad sighing, "It's hard to be loved by idiots," while holding his head in his hands.

The publication was met with protests in Paris and by lawsuits filed by Muslim groups. In response, "the magazine's publisher and lawyers argued they had the right to freedom of expression and criticized the Muslim groups for trying to prosecute a crime of blasphemy."[19] Ultimately, the judge in the case acquitted *Charlie Hebdo* in 2007.

Paris offices of Charlie Hebdo *prior to the November 2011 fire-bombing*[20]

The first terrorist attack on *Charlie Hebdo* occurred four years later, on November 2, 2011, when the newspapers offices were fire-bombed. The assault occurred early in the morning, shortly after 1 am. There were no injuries, but the offices were so badly damaged that the weekly was forced to relocate.

The inciting cause for the fire-bombing was the paper's publication of a special issue of the periodical, re-dubbed *Charia Hebdo* for the occasion. The title was a play on the Arabic term *shari'a*, referring to the code known as the "Islamic Way." The issue was purportedly "guest-edited" by none other than the prophet Muhammad himself. A caricature of Muhammad on the cover threatened the reader with "100 lashes if you don't die laughing."[21] Inside, among other things, was an editorial by "Muhammad" on halal drinks (drinks permissible under Islamic law), as well as a section covering Islamic veils, which had been recently banned in France.[22]

After the bombing, the editor-in-chief stated, "We no longer have a newspaper. All our equipment has been destroyed or has melted. We could not put a paper together today, but we will do everything possible to produce one next week. Whatever happens, we'll do it. There is no question of giving up."[23]

The cover of the paper's next edition responded overtly, albeit somewhat gently, to the attack by depicting a "male cartoonist kissing a Muslim man on the lips, with the caption 'Love is stronger than hate.'"[24]

Charlie Hebdo stall at a March 2012 Book Fair

The following year, in September 2012, the newspaper went on to publish cartoons ridiculing a naked Muhammad posed in pornographic positions. The weekly offered a short justification in the same issue asserting that freedom of speech should have no limits. The decision, however, led France to put its embassies on alert worldwide, and it also drew an unusual rebuke from the U. S. White House, whose spokesman Jim Carney asserted, "We don't question the right of something like this to be published, we just question the judgment behind the decision to publish it."[25]

The 11th district of Paris shortly after the shooting at the headquarters of Charlie Hebdo[26]

Editorial director Stéphane Charbonnier received death threats in 2012 and was extended police protection, yet *Charlie Hebdo* would continue to publish cartoons of the prophet.

At last, "foreign minister Laurent Fabius asked editors: 'Is it really sensible or intelligent to pour fuel on the fire?'" To this Gerard Biard, editor-in-chief, replied, "A newspaper is not a weapon of war."[27]

Biard would be away from the offices during the January 2015 attack, but Charbonnier was among those who died.

CHAPTER THREE

A Tale of Two *Charlies:*

"Free Speech Martyr" or "Childish Muslim Baiter"?

Memorial to the victims of the 2015 massacre, Toulon, France[28]

The hashtag #JeSuisCharlie went viral on social media worldwide almost immediately after the massacre on January 7, 2015. On January 11, as many as four million people marched in a show of unity with *Charlie Hebdo* in Paris, "the most marchers ever recorded in a nation that knows a thing or two about mass protests."[29] Despite these and other overwhelming shows of solidarity with the newspaper in the wake of the terrorist attack, there were many who refused to champion the paper's cause, or who did so with reservations or qualifications.

The reasons why particular individuals and groups might not wish to identify themselves with the newspaper so closely as to declare "I am Charlie" were several.

First, there were those who blamed *Charlie* in a manner that was somewhat akin to blaming a provocatively dressed women for inciting her own rape. After both the 2011 fire-bombing and the 2015 massacre, a minority in the media implied, some with greater and some with lesser subtlety, that *Charlie Hebdo* had "baited" Islamic extremists into taking violent action against the newspaper and could hardly have been surprised by the results. While no one from a major media outlet said outright that an anthropomorphized "Charlie" had "asked" for it, the inference was there, just waiting to be made. What most did agree about, though, was that when the news broke of first the 2011 bombing and then the 2015 murders, no one needed to look far for a motive.

Following the 2011 attack on the weekly's offices, Bruce Crumley in a *Time* magazine article entitled "Firebombed French Paper Is No Free Speech Martyr," negotiated an uneasy position between blaming and expressing sympathy for the victim. Crumley's article opens with this outraged exclamation:

> Okay, so can we finally stop with the idiotic, divisive, and destructive efforts by "majority sections" of Western nations to bait Muslim members with petulant, futile demonstrations that "they" aren't going to tell "us" what can and can't be done in free societies? Because not only are such Islamophobic antics futile and childish, but they also openly beg for the very violent responses from extremists their authors claim to proudly defy in the name of common good. What common good is served by creating more division and anger, and by tempting belligerent reaction?
>
> The difficulty in answering that question is also what's making it hard to have much sympathy for the French satirical newspaper firebombed this morning, after it

published another stupid and totally unnecessary edition mocking Islam.

Crumley's characterization of "Charlie" as a "petulant" child acting out simply to show that no one can tell "him" how to act cuts two ways. On one hand, it taps into a major motive behind the overwhelming *support* behind the weekly in 2015—its apparent status as an innocent martyr to free speech. On the other hand, it paints the paper's motives as selfish, stupid, and ultimately destructive, both to itself and to the larger society around it.[30]

The author's additional claim that *Charlie* was Islamophobic was one that had been made before, and it was one that would continue to be leveled at the newspaper by critics up to and after the 2015 massacre.

Unity March in Paris attended by approximately 1.6 million people, January 11, 2015[31]

Iranian-born commentator and activist Maryam Namazie, despite having significant reservations about the newspaper as a whole, insisted that it was essential to stand behind *Charlie Hebdo* regardless, on the grounds that one has to make a simple choice:

> *Charlie Hebdo* or the firebombers? You can't side with both.
>
> Whether you like or dislike *Charlie Hebdo*'s political position is irrelevant. It's just as irrelevant as what the woman who was raped was wearing or the nature of the "crime" committed by the person facing execution—that is if you agree that rape, execution and firebombing a publication for expressing a point of view are wrong, irrespective of the circumstances."[32]

Namazie's opening words recall the logically fallacious but famous line about terrorism uttered by then-President George W. Bush, "You're either with us or against us." But they also recall, in a simplistic way, the legendary quote on free speech spuriously attributed to the French Enlightenment philosopher Voltaire by a 20th-century biographer, a line that would move across social media like a wave after the 2015 attack on *Charlie Hebdo*: "I do not agree with what you have to say, but I'll defend to the death your right to say it."[33]

The logic is clear: if a person supports the principles of free speech that *Charlie Hebdo* invokes to license its satirical content, then he must support the weekly regardless of what he thinks of that content.

The building in which Charlie Hebdo*'s offices were located at the time of the 2015 attack*[34]

It was one thing to use inflammatory language like Crumley's after the 2011 terrorist attack that had hurt only papers, furnishings, and computers. But in 2015, when the losses were counted in human lives, it was quite another.

Nevertheless, we hear at least faint echoes of Crumley's argument in the media in January 2015, too. For example, in an interview with a Canadian outlet, Imam Sikander Hashmi contemplated the terrorists' motives in the more recent incident:

> What would prompt these thugs and criminals to actually go ahead and do this at this time? One indication could be that the newspaper actually took on ISIS just this week with the headline that there haven't been any attacks in France. There was a character turbaned with a Kalashnikov saying, "Wait, we still have until the end of January to extend our wishes." They also tweeted about the ISIS kingpin, Abu Bakr al-Baghdadi, giving him best wishes.
>
> This suggests, in my mind at least, that this could probably have more to do with ISIS and their feelings being hurt as opposed to the cartoons about the Prophet Muhammad, peace be upon him. This could be a case that perhaps they're using that as some sort of cover excuse to gain sympathy, which clearly has not worked, because most of the world is enraged and it would be very disingenuous and treacherous of them, even more so beyond the terrible act that they committed, to actually be using the Prophet Muhammad as an excuse for this type of action.

The implication that *Charlie Hebdo* invited the attack with its taunting cartoon cannot be dismissed. Although the Imam goes on to condemn the massacre itself, evincing disgust that the terrorists might have been using the magazine's depiction of the Prophet Muhammad "treacherously" as a "cover excuse to gain sympathy," he does nothing to dispel the widely held idea that the weekly, too, has treated Muhammad and the Islamic faith treacherously, though in its case by publishing its cartoons.

The Imam allows the newspaper to occupy the position of victim while refusing to grant it the status of a martyr.

Activist and commentator Sally Kohn carefully negotiated her own distinction between the two "Charlies" in the wake of the 2015 massacre:

> In the aftermath of the heinous attacks on the satirical newspaper *Charlie Hebdo* in France, many are tweeting and

writing in solidarity: Je suis Charlie. But I'm not. Because I am not Charlie.

Of course, I unequivocally support the right to free speech. Period. And I also believe in choosing to exercise that right responsibly and respectfully. That's why I would not have published cartoons depicting Prophet Mohammed, insulting 1.6 billion Muslims worldwide in the process (and no, I wouldn't have published many of *Charlie Hebdo*'s cartoons insulting Judaism and Christianity, either).

In no way should this be taken—as it has been by some on Twitter—to suggest that I somehow condone the killings of *Charlie Hebdo*'s staff. That's a ridiculously insulting idea and just plain wrong. It's possible to honor and protect the free speech rights of publications like *Charlie Hebdo* while simultaneously believing such cartoons are unnecessarily disrespectful and offensive.[35]

In Kohn's view, one can simultaneously see the newspaper as a martyr to free speech and condemn it for how it chooses to exercise its right to speak.

"I am not Charlie—"Je ne suis pas Charlie."

This phrase, in different variations, would make its way onto social media sites, placards, and posters to challenge with a variety of minority opinions the ubiquitous #JeSuisCharlie.

Milder than the Montreal sign reproduced in chapter 1 that reads, "And I blaspheme if I want to," was a sign carried by a male demonstrator at a unity rally in Strasbourg, France, on January 11, 2015, which read, "Je Suis Libre," or "I am free."[36] The sign did not equate him directly with "Charlie" but rather with the principles of free speech that were implicated in the tragedy. Another placard held at a rally in Lyon, France, on January 15 preserved the "Je Suis Charlie" but made the reason for its bearers' identification with the paper clear by adding, "Pour la liberté d'expression," or "For freedom of expression."

More overtly critical was a poster (available in three sizes) from the U. K. company The Keep Calm-O-Matic, which proclaimed, "Je Ne Suis Pas Charlie parce que je ne suis pas Islamaphobe!" or "I am not Charlie because I am not an Islamaphobe!"

Still others impugned not *Charlie Hebdo* but rather the uncritical, sheep-like following that they believed the massacre had spawned. Flickr user Tjebbe van Tijen declared "Je ne suis pas Charlie," and then went on to rail against the hypocrisy of the prominent figures who now stood to support the fallen staff of the paper:

> Most of the supportive crowds outside of France have NO idea with what was the "bad taste fun" that Charlie Hebdo has been poking for decades at ALL AUTHORITY... not just at authoritarian islamists. Those who have been vilified on many occasions by Charlie Hebdo take their revenge now by praising their dead former adversaries for their "courageous defence of the freedom of expression": [former French President Nicolas] Sarkozy, [French politician] Marine Le Pen, [French President François] Hollande, ...

In the accompanying image appeared a mirror version of the words "Je Suis Charlie," which the user intended to symbolically "counter the 'recuperation' of Charlie Hebdo with the weapon of the *détournement*, turning around or highjacking."[37] Turnabout is fair play, as the saying goes.

One of the most poignant reworkings of the slogan took the form of the tag #JeSuisAhmed, which sought to memorialize one of the two policemen, Ahmed Merabet, who died during the attacks on *Charlie Hebdo*'s offices. With all the media's and popular focus on the seeming martyrdom of the periodical's editor and cartoonists who were the target of the terrorist's attack, the two police officers who stood to defend them at the scene and became collateral casualities attracted far less attention. This was despite the fact that the morality of their actions, unlike the newspaper's, could not be called into question.

Je ne suis pas Charlie.
Je suis Ahmed.

I am Ahmed the dead cop.
Charlie ridiculed my faith and culture and i died defending
his right to do so.

Image posted to Flickr January 2015 by Arivan Miculis Reigota, entitled "Against Terrorism. Against Xenophobia. For Life."[38]

A deceptively simple black-and-white slide posted to Flickr reads, "Je ne suis pas Charlie. Je suis Ahmed." In smaller text below, as if in a whisper, "Ahmed" speaks from the grave: "I am Ahmed the dead cop. Charlie ridiculed my faith and culture and I died defending his right to do so." The source of the English language text was a tweet made by Dyab Abou Jahjah on January 8, 2015. Within four days it had been retweeted more than 39,000 times.

In a personal and emotional way, the slide captures with incredible nuance the distinction that Kohn had made between the *Charlie* who stood as a champion of free speech and the *Charlie* who unrepentantly satirized the Islamic (and other) faiths.

In an interview published in *The Huffington Post* U. K., Ahmed Merabet's brother Malek condemned the terrorists, but he also condemned Islamophobes who fail to distinguish between Muslim extremists and non-extremists. Describing his brother as "a Muslim" who was "killed by people who pretend to be Muslims," Malek went on to say, "I address myself now to all the racists, Islamophobes and antisemites. One must not confuse extremists with Muslims. Mad people have neither colour or religion."

It is impossible to know for sure whether Merabet intends for us to see *Charlie Hebdo* as one of the Islamophobes whom he condemns. However, when he states that his brother was "proud to represent the police and of defending the values of the Republic—liberty, equality, fraternity"—but that his death, ultimately, was "a waste," one cannot help but wonder if he, too, intends for us to see that there is not one *Charlie*, but two.[39]

CHAPTER FOUR

Muhammad and Jihad —

Does "God Need No Defense"?

Islamic Protest in Hyde Park, Sydney[40]

If we agree that we need to distinguish between two "Charlies"—that is, between the *Charlie Hebdo* that championed free speech and the *Charlie Hebdo* that exercised it—then we must agree to do the same when it comes to the Muslims who have taken action against the newspaper's satires of Islam.

Although Crumley's 2011 *Time* article reads at times like hyperbole, there is, at the very least, a kernel of truth within it—the magazine has "baited" Muslims, both radical and non-radical alike. And it has done so throughout much of its recent history. If we look back to 2006 (the reprinting of the Danish cartoons) and 2011 (the special issue "guest-edited" by the prophet Muhammad), we note a range of responses to the paper's exercise of free speech from within the

Islamic community. While extremists reacted by bombing the paper's offices, more moderate Muslims spoke out against the newspaper, staged protests, and filed lawsuits in the French courts.

French law provides protections against speech (written or otherwise) that provokes violence, hatred, or discrimination. But in executing the law, the courts have had to straddle a fine line that requires them to distinguish between speech that is anti-Islamic (directed against the religious tenets of Islam) and anti-Muslim (directed against the Muslim community itself). In general, the courts have found that "it was acceptable to debate or even to insult Islam as a religious doctrine, as long as a speaker did not provoke hatred against Muslims as a group."[41] Anything that does not violate this provision is therefore protected as free speech under French law.

After the 2011 fire-bombing attack on *Charlie Hebdo*, editor-in-chief Gerard Biard made clear that his publication was committed to working within the limits of free speech as the nation defined it— but within those limits alone. Biard said, "We're a newspaper that respects French law. Now, if there's a law that is different in Kabul or Riyadh, we're not going to bother ourselves with respecting it."[42]

Inevitably, this position taken by the weekly placed it at odds with fundamentalist interpretations of the Islamic *shari'a*, or the "Islamic Way." It is this set of codes, and the laws that have arisen from it, that have "shaped much of the interaction of modern Islam with the non-Islamic world."[43]

The words of Associate Justice of the U. S. Supreme Court Robert H. Jackson on the Islamic laws of the Middle East are as relevant to France as they are to America:

> In its source, its scope and its sanctions, the law of the Middle East is the antithesis of Western law. . . . To the American, the most fundamental of differences lies in the relation between law and religion. In the West, even those countries which do not accept the idea of rigid separation

of church and state still regard the legal system as mainly a secular concern in which expediency plays a large part. . . .

Islamic law, on the contrary, finds its chief source in the will of Allah as revealed to the Prophet Muhammad. It contemplates one community of the faithful, though they may be of various tribes and in widely separated locations. Religion, not nationalism or geography, is the proper cohesive force. The state itself is subordinate to the Qur'ān, which leaves little room for additional legislation, none for criticism or dissent. . . .

It is not possible to separate political or juristic theories from the teachings of the Prophet, which establish rules of conduct concerning religious, domestic, social and political life. This results in a law of duties rather than of rights, of moral obligation binding on the individual, from which no earthly authority can relieve him, and which he disobeys at peril of his future life. . . . Americans do not accept the religious or philosophical foundations of Islamic law.[44]

Several features of the Middle Eastern Islamic law that Jackson sketches are in stark contrast to the French laws that Biard invoked in describing *Charlie Hebdo*'s stance on free speech: it is "a law of duty rather than rights"; it is a law not bounded by nation or geography but universally applied among all followers of the religion; and it is a law that cannot be overridden by the authorities of the secular state.

Abdurrahman Wahid, former President of Indonesia[45]

It is the extremist Middle Eastern form of Islamic law that has shaped western stereotypes. This version of the law, however, is the product of human interpretation, no less than the secular laws of the west are, and this interpretation is not the only, nor even the dominant, one. In the words of the late Kyai Haji Abdurrahman Wahid, President of Indonesia (the world's largest Muslim nation):

> In its original *Qur'anic* sense, the word *sharia* refers to "the way," the path to God, and not to formally codified Islamic law, which only emerged in the centuries following Muhammad's death. . . . [I]t is thus vital that we differentiate between the *Qur'an*—from which much of the raw material for producing Islamic law is derived—and the law itself. For while its revelatory inspiration is divine,

Islamic law is man-made and thus subject to human interpretation and revision.

On the one hand, *sharia*, properly understood, expresses and embodies perennial values. Islamic law, on the other hand, is the product of *ijtihad* (interpretation), which depends on circumstances (*al-hukm yadur ma'a al-'illah wujudan wa 'adaman*) and needs to be continuously reviewed in accordance with ever-changing circumstances. This is necessary to prevent Islamic law from becoming out of date, rigid, and noncorrelative, not only with Muslims' contemporary lives and conditions, but also with the underlying perennial values of *sharia* itself.[46]

In January 2015, a spokesperson from Yemen's Al-Qaida claimed responsibility for the murders at *Charlie Hebdo*. A statement released by the group stated that the attack's purpose was to revenge the prophet Muhammad, whom the weekly had repeatedly lampooned in its cartoons. As such, the statement recalls the words of the assailants that were recorded at the time of the attack: "We have avenged the Prophet Muhammad! We have killed Charlie Hebdo!"

If we were to judge *Charlie Hebdo* following the Pakistani Shari'a Court's legal interpretation of what it means to "Defil[e] the name of Muhammad," then we would quite obviously need to find the newspaper guilty. This offense the Court defines as follows:

> reviling or insulting the Prophet in writing or speech; speaking profanely or contemptuously about him or his family; attacking the Prophet's dignity and honor in an abusive manner; vilifying him or making an ugly face when his name is mentioned; showing enmity or hatred towards him, his family, his companions, and the Muslims; accusing, or slandering the Prophet and his family, including spreading evil reports about him or his family; defaming the Prophet; refusing the Prophet's jurisdiction or judgment in any manner; rejecting the Sunnah; showing disrespect, contempt for or rejection of the rights of Allah and His Prophet or rebelling against Allah and His Prophet.

Under Pakistani law, the penalty for this crime is death.[47]

It is not too difficult to see how an extremist might seek to take this punishment out of the court's hands and into his own, since the Islamic duty of *jihad* requires that individuals exert themselves on behalf of God's cause. On the personal level, it requires the individual to undertake a struggle to follow the righteous path that God has ordained. On the level of the unified "nation" of Islam, it demands the encouragement of the good and the correction of evil, as well as the defense of Islam. In the time of Muhammad himself, and later in the name of his example, *jihad* has been used to justify the use of a range of weapons—including political, economic, and deadly ones.

A well-known case that is commonly invoked to parallel *Charlie Hebdo*'s is that of *The Satanic Verses* author Salman Rushdie. In 1989, Iran's Ayatollah Khomeini issued a fatwa sentencing Rushdie to death for blasphemy and appealed to all Muslims to kill him, along with everyone who had been involved in the novel's publication. Rushdie's irreverent depiction of a character taken to be a figure for the prophet Muhammad was deemed particularly offensive by many Muslims.

A fatwa is "an opinion made by a judicial/religious scholar (a mufti) on a legal, civil, or religious matter."[48] In other words, it is an interpretation of the law, though normally the opinion is not binding on the Muslim people. The Ayatollah's fatwa, however, could be seen by some as a mandate, or at least a precedent, for those within the Islamic community to take similar action against anyone who lampooned the Prophet, including the staff of *Charlie Hebdo*.

Rushdie made a statement announcing his solidarity with the newspaper after the 2015 massacre. He wrote, "I stand with Charlie Hebdo, as we all must, to defend the art of satire, which has always been a force for liberty and against tyranny, dishonesty, and stupidity. . . . [R]eligious totalitarianism has caused a deadly mutation in the heart of Islam and we see the tragic consequences in Paris today."[49]

Such extremist interpretations of Islamic law as Khomeini's and the Pakistani Shari'a Court's are not ones that the majority of Muslims share. Former Indonesian President Wahid, for example, turns the fundamentalists' charges of blasphemy back upon them when he writes, "Those who presume to fully grasp God's will, and dare to impose by force their own limited understanding of this upon others, are essentially equating themselves with God and are unwittingly engaged in blasphemy."[50]

Kai Hafez, an Associate Research Fellow of the German Institute for Middle East Studies, further notes that in cases of blasphemy or apostasy, "the Qur'an recommends punishments only for 'the beyond' but not for life on earth." Moreover, the Qur'an "lays down several freedom rights, including the freedom of expression."[51]

As Wahid says succinctly, "God needs no defense."[52]

CHAPTER FIVE

Charlie's Defense:

We Mock "Ideas not Men"

The Grand Mosque in Paris[53]

The French courts similarly uphold the idea that God needs no defense. In their interpretation and application of the law, speech that criticizes or insults the Islamic faith is protected, so long as it does not provoke violence, hatred, or discrimination toward the Muslim community at large.

The limits of free speech in France were tested in 2006 when Paris's Grand Mosque and other Muslim groups leveled criminal charges against *Charlie Hebdo* after it reprinted the Danish caricatures of Muhammad with an original cover illustration.

Specifically, the groups charged that the weekly was guilty of "publicly abusing a group of people because of their religion."[54]

Charlie Hebdo's director at the time, Etienne Val, responded to the lawsuit by claiming "that the cartoons he published did not constitute a hate-speech crime, because they had targeted 'ideas, not men.'" As he told the *Wall Street Journal*, the satire was directed toward "not believers but religion when it is used as an alibi to perpetrate terrorist acts." He further expressed the opinion that, "When religion leaves the private sphere, it becomes an ideology like any other, and must accept to be criticized with the same virulence as any other ideology. That is the very essence of democracy."[55]

A key element of the newspaper's defense involved establishing that the cartoons it published targeted only extremist Muslims, rather than Muslims as a whole. The weekly's position was that the cartoons thereby "contributed to an ongoing public debate."[56]

The cover that *Charlie Hebdo* published to accompany the twelve Danish cartoons does frame the comics within a careful context that appears to support this assertion. Captioned "Muhammad and the Fundamentalists," the cover illustration shows the prophet holding his head in his hands while sighing, "It's hard to be loved by idiots."[57] Here Muhammad himself is made to condemn the extremists who act in his name—but only those extremists. It is not Muslims generally who are "idiotic" but the Muslim fundamentalists who interpret Islamic law in "idiotic" ways.

More problematic, though, are some of the reproduced Danish cartoons that appeared in the same issue. As Erik Bleich argues,

> The claims by the Danish prosecutor, by French courts, and by one of the cartoonists that the illustrations target only a portion of Muslims strain credibility. In the context of post-9/11 Western Europe, identifying Muhammad with terrorism or violent misogyny taps into and aggravates widespread prejudice about Muslims. Moreover, unlike [controversial French author Michel] Houellebecq's statements that denigrate Islamic

doctrine, these caricatures summarize Muslims as a group, rather than Islam as a religion. By their nature, these depictions cannot distinguish between subcategories and have the effect of lumping together all followers of Muhammad.[58]

Although some of the Danish cartoons were relatively benign, others were viciously satirical. The reason for this diversity among the twelve cartoons arose from the context within which they were commissioned by the culture editor of *Jyllands-Posten*, Flemming Rose. Like *Charlie Hebdo*'s Val, Rose explicitly sought to position the illustrations within the context of public debate when legal proceedings were earlier initiated against the Danish periodical.

Rose explained that his motive for commissioning the illustrations was to assess the extent to which artists in Denmark might be self-censoring when it came to Islamic subject matter, presumably out of fear that they might outrage the nation's Muslim population. Rose "asked all forty-two members of the Danish newspaper illustrators' union to draw images of Muhammad, as they envisioned him." Twelve took part, and it was this collection of illustrations that would go on to spark an international furor.

Rose's conclusion from the experiment was "that fear, whether warranted or not, was creating a climate of self-censorship in Denmark with regard to important issues surrounding 'the most important cultural meeting of our times, the one between Islam and the secular, western society with its roots in Christianity.'"[59]

One of the cartoons expressed the artistic community's fear of self-censorship vividly; it offered "a depiction of a frightened-looking cartoonist huddled over a portrait titled 'Muhammad' as he drew."[60] Another illustration was a now-infamous caricature of Muhammad with a turban-bomb. In its defense, its illustrator explained that it was not meant to signify that Muhammad himself was a terrorist but sought to "satirize the hijacking of Islam by violent extremists."[61]

In France, the court in March 2007 acquitted *Charlie Hebdo*, saying it had "found no sign of a 'deliberate intention of directly and gratuitously offending the Muslim community.'" In making its judgment, the court "emphasized such specific factors as the 'context' of the drawings, that *Charlie-Hebdo* 'is a satirical paper … that no one is obliged to buy or read,' and that caricatures are by definition intended to go 'beyond good taste.'" [62]

Although the court recognized that the individual cartoons had to be considered separately from one another, their publication in a satirical publication had to be recognized as shaping their meaning. The court "argued that in such outlets, deliberate provocation and exaggeration can be an instrument of social and political critique which—within limits—must be protected expression." While the court acknowledged that the turban-bomb cartoon was "shocking, even hurtful," it found that the image could not be considered outside of the context of the larger issue and thus did not meet the test for hate-speech crimes. [63]

The French court's decision offered a wide berth for the satirical paper, and ultimately it made defensible *Charlie Hebdo*'s choice to continue publishing provocatively satirical cartoons of Muhammad and other Islamic subjects. Adding further weight to the court's decision was its confirmation on appeal. The appellate court judged that the illustrations "were clearly aimed at a fraction and not at the entirety of the Muslim community." [64]

Undoubtedly a great many Muslims had been offended by the illustrations, both on religious grounds and based on their perception that the French court had marginalized their community and its concerns. Whether *Charlie Hebdo*'s publication of the cartoons, however, actually rose to the level of provoking a generalized hatred or discrimination against Muslims as a whole is harder to assess.

To the extent that *Charlie Hebdo* indeed published the issue with the Danish cartoons in the spirit of promoting public debate, they scored a significant victory for western ideals. As Paul Marshall and Nina Shea write, "If we acquiesce in the legitimacy of repressing religious debate, then we boost those who are or would be our enemies . . . In abiding by such strictures ourselves, we politically disarm ourselves by making discussion, debate, and analysis of

Islam and its various interpretations out of bounds."[65] It is the "Charlie" who championed these ideals who would take his position as a free speech hero and martyr after the 2015 massacre; it is this "Charlie" who would inspire the viral meme "Je Suis Charlie."

And yet, as Bleich reminds us, "just because it is legally permitted to publish outrageous material does not mean that it is wise or ethical to do so, nor that there may not be consequences for that decision."[66] This more ethically and pragmatically suspect version of "Charlie" would take his place in the post-massacre debates as well, spawning counter-memes refusing to grant the weekly the status of either hero or martyr.

CHAPTER SIX

"Je Suis Charlie"

A cartoon tribute to Charlie Hebdo[67]

The two "Charlies" who emerged during the 2006 lawsuit over the reprinted Danish cartoons returned to the public eye in January 2015.

The morning of the 7th, two armed gunmen stormed into *Charlie Hebdo*'s offices and killed ten people, including eight members of the paper's staff, a caretaker, and a visitor. Three police officers and four people at a Jewish supermarket also fell victim to the terrorists during the three-day spree that began that day. In total, seventeen people died, and many more were injured. Al-Qaida claimed responsibility for the attack.

When the terrorists who forced their way into the newspaper's offices proudly declared they had "killed Charlie Hebdo," they unwittingly set the stage for the triumphant return of the "Charlie" who was the heroic champion of free speech.

The attack on the paper was dubbed by some "the darkest day in the history of the French press." Cartoonists and journalists from around the world came out in solidarity with *Charlie Hebdo*. The day of the attack, the Australian cartoonist David Pope tweeted a moving image. In it, he depicted a terrorist, garbed from head to toe in black and holding a smoking rifle, standing above the body of an artist lying in a pool of blood, a pair of glasses and an illustration scattered beside him. The terrorist says punningly in his defense, "He drew first."[68]

Pope's cartoon poignantly recalls editor Stéphane Charbonnier's statement in 2012 that "a drawing has never killed anyone."[69] Charbonnier died in the 2015 massacre.

In the wake of the attack, the paper's website went eerily quiet. No hyperlinks appeared on the home page.

A somber, mournful black screen, with a strong, upraised hand clenching a thick pencil as its only graphic, announced at the top in all caps, "JE SUIS CHARLIE" ("I am Charlie").

Below, blocks of headline text declared:

> PARCE QUE LE CRAYON SERRA TOUJOURS AU DESSUS DE LA BARBARIE...
>
> *[Because the pen is always above barbarism . . .]*
>
> PARCE QUE LA LIBERTÉ EST UN DROIT UNIVERSEL...
>
> *[Because freedom is a universal right . . .]*
>
> PARCE QUE VOUS NOUS SOUTENEZ...
>
> *[Because you support us . . .]*
>
> NOUS, CHARLIE SORTIRONS VOTRE JOURNAL MERCREDI PROCHAIN!
>
> *[We, Charlie will publish your newspaper next Wednesday!]*

An inset box proclaimed, "CHARLIE HEBDO LES JOURNAL DES SURVIVANTS, MERCREDI 14/1" ("Charlie Hebdo the Journal of Survivors, Wednesday, 1/14"), citing the date of the promised forthcoming issue.

A public tribute to Charlie Hebdo[70]

Within hours of the home page's posting, the meme "JE SUIS CHARLIE" went viral worldwide as hundreds, thousands, and finally millions began to gather for vigils and unity marches designed to show their grief for, and solidarity with, *Charlie Hebdo.* The lights on the Eiffel Tower were extinguished in respect for the victims. Its famous words, "'Liberte, Egalite, Fraternite," were "obscured by all the posters, banners, candles and bouquets" memorializing the fallen. As one writer put it, instead "we now see 'Je suis Charlie,'" and even "the statue of the French national figurehead, Marianne, standing proudly above that great motto of the Revolution . . . had become 'Charlie' too. As a three-dimensional grand tableau, this was one hell of a cartoon." [71]

"Graffiti created on the wall of the former Blind Tiger Club on the corner of Grand Parade and Kingswood Street - in Brighton, England, UK - during January 2015"[72]

Supporters from around the globe identified themselves with "Charlie" and with the principles of free speech for which the newspaper stood by carrying placards bearing the slogan, "Je Suis Charlie," by placing cards and signs carrying the words at memorial sites, and by spray-painting graffiti on walls to honor the paper. Soon the signs were being mass-printed, and T-shirts bearing the same words appeared.

A tribute to Charlie Hebdo [73]

Tributes were painted on quotidian objects—bicycles, pencils and pencil cups.

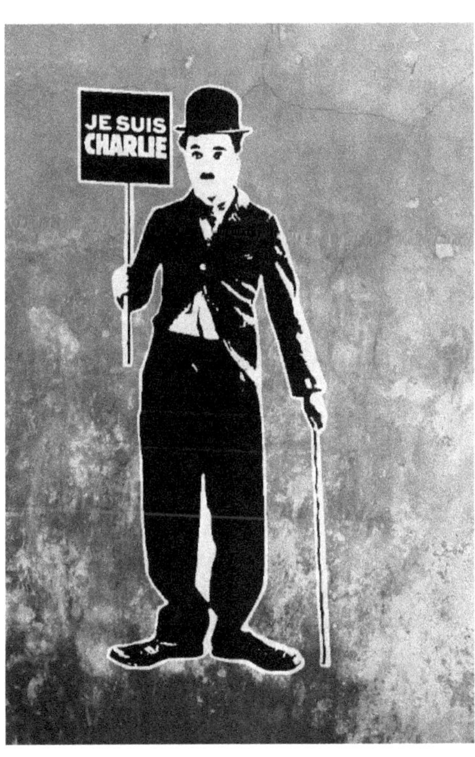

A tribute to Charlie Hebdo[74]

Cartoonists and other artists posted tributes via sites like Flickr, Twitter, and Tumblr. Some depicted the silent-film star Charlie Chaplin, known for his often socially critical slapstick humor, carrying a "Je Suis Charlie" sign.

A tribute to Charlie Hebdo[75]

It seemed that everyone, even down to a garden gnome, supported the paper.

#JeSuisCharlie quickly became one of the most popular "news-related" Twitter hashtags ever: "At its peak on Thursday evening [January 8th, the day after the massacre], there were nearly 6,500 tweets per minute with the hashtag. As of late Friday, there had been more than 5 million tweets using the #JeSuisCharlie hashtag."[76]

On January 10, 2015, writer Brian Reede invited readers of *The Mirror* to "Turn to Twitter and Defeat the Terrorists." He explained:

> Everyone can be Charlie. If you really want to be him, all you need to do is post one of the cartoons on Twitter or Facebook, and if everyone does the same it will travel the world hundreds of millions of times. Then do the same with the cartoon on next week's front page of *Charlie Hebdo*.

> It would mean that the terrorists had ended up promoting the joke. They would be the ones responsible for making the world laugh at their god.[77]

Pope Francis[78]

But there were other, minority voices as well, voices that refused to stand with the newspaper and say, "I am Charlie." Perhaps the most famous voice belonged to Pope Francis.

Besides leading a mass to honor the victims of the massacre, Francis joined four Imams in issuing a statement "warning that the world is a dangerous place without freedom of expression but urging the media to be respectful of religion."

As others had done after the fire-bombing of the newspaper's offices in 2011, Francis implied that *Charlie Hebdo,* in the exercise of its freedom of speech, had baited its Muslim attackers. A week after the massacre, when some of the victims' bodies were being laid to rest, he offered a joking analogy: "'If my good friend Doctor Gasparri [who organises the Pope's trips] speaks badly of my mother, he can expect to get punched,' he said, throwing a pretend punch at the doctor, who was standing beside him."[79]

"You can't make fun of faith," the Pope said.[80]

Salman Rushdie defended *Charlie Hebdo,* saying, "The thing that I really resent is the way in which these, our dead comrades . . . have been almost immediately vilified and called racists and I don't know what else. . . . You can dislike *Charlie Hebdo.* . . . But the fact that you dislike them has nothing to do with their right to speak."[81]

Whether one sides with Salman Rushdie or the Pope in choosing to see *Charlie Hebdo* as a heroic champion of free speech, a Muslim-baiter, or both, there can be no doubt that neither "Charlie" nor free speech died in the terrorist attack on January 7, 2015.

The surviving members of the paper's staff, who would meet again only two days after the massacre to start work on the next issue, received an outpouring not just of moral support but also financial backing. The newspaper *Liberation* allowed *Charlie Hebdo* to set up offices temporarily in their space. The French government pledged €1 million to enable the paper to continue functioning, while Google donated $300,000 "to *Charlie Hebdo* to ensure it's not silenced." The Press and Pluralism association started a fundraising website that had raised $600,000 within a few days.[82] A Crowdfunding campaign was started to support the paper and the families of the victims. As of January 15, it had collected roughly €149,000 from more than 5,000 participants.[83]

In an interview, *Charlie Hebdo* columnist Patrick Pelloux declared, "The paper will continue because they didn't win," saying that his colleagues "didn't die for nothing."[84]

Because of the groundswell of popular support, *Charlie Hebdo* announced that it would print 1 million copies of its "Survivors" edition on Wednesday, January 14, 2015, compared to its usual run of no more than 60,000. The paper would increase this number to 5 million when the first print run sold out within minutes. The company's distributor reassured the public, "We will keep printing every day to satisfy demand."[85] The paper was to be distributed to countries where it is not normally sold due to lack of demand, including the United States. It would be translated into Italian and Turkish print editions, as well as English, Arabic, and Spanish digital editions.[86]

The demand for the issue was so great that it spawned two new social media hashtags: #Jaimoncharlie ("I have my Charlie") and #SelfieCharlie. French readers who were able to secure copies on the date of issue posted photographs of themselves, paper in hand.[87]

The newspaper's cover image went viral instantly. It depicts a turbaned, sad-faced Muhammad directly facing the viewer, a tear falling from one eye. In his hand he holds a sign that reads, "JE SUIS CHARLIE." Above his head are the words, "TOUT EST PARDONNÉ," "All is forgiven."

As L. V. Anderson notes, the meaning of the cartoon is ambiguous: "Was Charlie forgiving Muhammad, or was Muhammad forgiving Charlie? Either way, was the forgiveness sarcastic or sincere?"

Perhaps an equally important question to ask is this: what is Muhammad saying about himself by holding in his hand the same sign borne by Charlie's supporters, by identifying himself with the magazine?

The illustrator, Luz, explained his own conception of the image:

> I had this idea that I was stuck on: to draw my caricature of Mohammed, the one that had started all the chatter. And to do him holding a "Je Suis Charlie" sign. It made me laugh. It was my last-ditch effort. So I drew my little drawing, and I looked at his face, and it made me laugh. I saw this character who had been used in spite of himself by nut jobs who set shit on fire, by terrorists. Humorless assholes: That's what these terrorists are. Of course everything is forgiven, my man Mohammed. We can overcome, because I managed to draw you. I showed my drawing to Richard Malka, then to [editor] Gérard Biard, and then we cried. Because we had it, a cover that looked like us, and that didn't look like everyone else or like the symbols that have been imposed on us over the last few days. Not a cover with bullet holes, but just a cover that makes us laugh.[88]

Luz represents the cartoon as a display of triumphant defiance, an embodiment of the paper's victory over the "Humorless" terrorists who had used violence to avenge earlier depictions of Muhammad, all in the prophet's name. But it's also an image that communicates forgiveness and builds a bridge between *Charlie Hebdo* and the larger Muslim community of believers by sending the message that the Islamic community "is Charlie," too.

The cover thus would seem intended by the artist to communicate the same message that the 2006 cover illustration accompanying the Danish cartoons had. There, Muhammad held his head in his hands, lamenting that "it is hard to be loved by idiots"—idiots explicitly identified as fundamentalist Muslims in the caption. At the same time, the "Survivors" cover could be seen to capture the spirit of forgiveness that is embodied in the 2011 post-fire-bombing cover, which showed a cartoonist embracing a Muslim beneath the caption, 'Love is stronger than hate.'"

The cover the magazine finally decided upon was far less provocative than others it had considered. According to Luz, one such idea was to depict "portraits of Charlie's murdered cartoonists with the headline, 'We are God.'" [89]

Regarding the cover that was finally chosen, Luz said, "It wasn't the cover the world wanted us to do. It wasn't the cover the terrorists wanted us to do. But it's ours. We drew Muhammad again. I'm sorry. But the Muhammad we drew is above all a fellow who is crying." [90]

For all its pathos, the cartoon's portrayal of the image of Muhammad, which spites the Islamic taboo against such representations, undercuts its potentially conciliatory message. As in the Danish cartoon issue, so too does the content within the pages of the paper itself.

A cartoon by one of the artists who died in the massacre shows "an Islamist cleric telling peers, 'Charlie Hebdo people shouldn't be touched . . . otherwise, they will pass for martyrs and, in paradise, those assholes are going to steal all our virgins!'" In another, a Muslim woman exposes herself to "a crowd of penis-nosed clerics looking on from inside the open garment." [91]

True to form, *Charlie Hebdo* did not only satirize Muslims in the issue but also the Catholic Church. "More people had turned out the previous Sunday to support their paper 'than for Mass,'" it said. [92] A cartoon depicts the Pope thinking, "My God, forgive these cocksuckers," as he gives a group of women communion. [93]

The issue's attacks on the Catholic Church, of course, did nothing to mitigate the perceived offensiveness of the Islamic subject matter that it contained. Muslims worldwide staged protests after the weekly's release. For example, at a protest in the Phillipines, a group of Muslims carried a large sign that read, "Vous êtes Charlie (You are Charlie)—Je Aime *[sic]* Mohammad (SAW) (#LoveMohammad (Saw))." Others carried signs that said, "You are Charlie—Respect Islam" and "YOU ARE CHARLIE—I AM MOHAMMAD." There were "banners waved that declared there would be no apology from the Islamic world for the Paris massacre." One sign even demanded, "FRANCE MUST APOLOGIZE."

In Cairo, a spokesperson for the Al-Azhar mosque remarked that the cover was "a blatant challenge to the feelings of Muslims who had sympathised with this newspaper." However, he asked Muslims to react by "showing tolerance, forgiveness and shedding light on the story of the prophet." Many feared the newspaper's cover would provoke further acts of violence.

Other Muslims protested the issue on the grounds that "their expressions of solidarity with *Charlie Hebdo* after last week's attack had been rebuffed."[94]

Certainly, the "Survivors" issue was not uncritical of the paper's many "newfound friends." Editor Biard offered appreciation and thanks to those who "sincerely and deeply 'are Charlie.' And we say screw the other ones, who couldn't give a toss anyway." He went on to decry those who in the past have labeled the paper's staff "Islamophobes, Christian-phobics, provocateurs, casters of oil on the fire, racists, you-had-it-coming." Biard took particular issue with "critics long equivocal about the threats Charlie faced: 'Yes, we condemn terrorism, *but*. Yes, threatening cartoonists with death isn't good, *but*. Yes, burning down a newspaper is bad, *but*.'"[95]

Biard's position recalls that of Maryam Namazie after the 2011 fire-bombing, when the Iranian activist had argued that one has to choose to support *Charlie Hebdo* or the terrorists since "You can't side with both." [96]

A tribute to the staffers who had died ends by thanking them on the grounds that

> you have left us ovations when you lived being booed; you died unloved so that we might finally be understood. Thanks to you, we even got one year of free postage from the postal service! Everyone wants to help us, to read us, to subscribe, to buy us a coffee, a drink, a ticket . . . You are

spoiling us long after your death, but now we know, we fear: When the hardship returns, it will return without you.[97]

Having lost their friends to tragedy, and then gained many more new ones from it, *Charlie Hebdo* pessimistically forecasts an eventual return of the derision and poverty that it has faced throughout its history.

If and when that day comes, the "Je Suis Charlie" choir will have many fewer voices speaking in unison, but one imagines that "Charlie" will use his voice to continue to speak his mind as freely, and as irreverently, as ever.

REFERENCES

[1]Photo credit: Pascal POGGI, "Paris Place de la république 3," 14 February 2014, via Flickr, Creative Commons Attribution.

[2]"Charlie Hebdo's mysterious last tweet before attack," *BBC Trending*, 7 January 2015.

[3]"Charlie Hebdo to print 1 million copies next week," *New York Post,* 8 January 2015.

[4]Dan Bilefsky and Maia de la Baume, "Terrorists Strike Charlie Hebdo Newspaper in Paris, Leaving 12 Dead," *New York Times,* 7 January 2015.

[5]"Read the New Issue of Charlie Hebdo in English," *The Daily Beast* 14 January 2015.

[6]Editorial Board, "The Charlie Hebdo Massacre in Paris," *New York Times*, 7 January 2015.

[7]Michael Holtz, "Charlie Hebdo: The French magazine's long history of polarization (+video)," *The Christian Science Monitor*, 7 January 2015.

[8]Photo credit: Olivier Ortelpa, "Paris, place de la Republique le 11 janvier 2015," 11 January, 2015, via Flickr, Creative Commons Attribution.

[9]*Frommer's Paris* 2013. Ed. Jennifer Polland. Hoboken, NJ: John Wiley & Sons, Inc., 2012.

[10]Photo credit: ollografik, "Hommage à Charlie hebdo place de la République," February 14, 2014, via Flickr, Creative Commons Attribution.

[11]Photo credit: Gerry Lauzon, "Rien à foutre," 7 January 2015, via Flickr, Creative Commons Attribution.

[12]Dan Bilefsky and Maia de la Baume, "Terrorists Strike Charlie

Hebdo Newspaper in Paris, Leaving 12 Dead," *NY Times*, 7 January 2015.

[13]"Charlie Hebdo: why was the satirical magazine attacked?," *MSN Magazine*, rpt. from theweek.co.uk, 7 January 2015.

[14]Photo credit: Pierre-Yves Beaudouin, "After the fire of the offices of the satirical French magazine Charlie Hebdo, November 2 2011, 62 boulevard Dayout, Paris, France," via Wikimedia Commons, Creative Commons License CC-BY-SA-3.0.

[15]"Global Cry in Defiance of Violence," *Winnipeg Free Press*, 8 January 2015.

[16]"Global Cry."

[17]Photo credit: David Monniaux, "Paris: Le journal 'Charlie Hebdo,'" via Wikimedia Commons, Creative Commons License, 8 February 2006.

[18]Erik Bleich, *The Freedom to Be Racist?: How the United States and Europe Struggle to Preserve Freedom and Combat Racism*, New York: Oxford University Press, 2011.

[19]Bleich, *The Freedom to Be Racist?*.

[20]Photo credit: David Monniaux, "Former headquarters of Charlie Hebdo - 2006-02-08," via Wikimedia Commons, Creative Commons License CC BY-SA 3.0.8, February 2006.

[21]Tom A. Peter, "'100 Lashes If You Don't Die Laughing' and 3 Other Muhammad Controversies," *The Christian Science Monitor*, 2 November 2011.

[22]Peter Allen, "Fire Attack on Magazine over Prophet Satire," *The Evening Standard* (London, England), 2 November 2011.

[23]Allen, "Fire Attack."

[24]"Charlie Hebdo: why was the satirical magazine attacked?," *MSN Magazine*, rpt. from theweek.co.uk, 7 January 2015.

[25]"White House Questioned French Magazine's 'Judgment' In 2012 For Publishing Naked Muhammad Cartoon," CBS Local DC, 7 January 2015.

[26]Photo credit: Thierry Caro, "Vue de la zone du 11e arrondissement interdite aux badauds par la police après la fusillade au siège de Charlie Hebdo, prise avec l'aide du journaliste de LCP Jérémie Hartmann," via Wikimedia Commons, Creative Commons License, 7 January 2015.

[27]Adam Sherwin, "Satirical French Magazine Was Warned Not to 'Pour Fuel on the Fire,'" *Cape Times* (South Africa), 9 January 2015.

[28]Photo credit: yves Tennevin, "Rassemblement de soutien à Charlie Hebdo - 7 janvier 2015 - Toulon - P1980318," 7 January 2015, via Flickr, Creative Commons Attribution.

[29]"Read the New Issue of Charlie Hebdo in English," *The Daily Beast*, 14 January 2015.

[30]Bruce Crumley, "Firebombed French Paper Is No Free Speech Martyr," *Time,* 2 November 2011.

[31]Photo credit: Yann Caradec, "Paris rally in support of the victims of the 2015 Charlie Hebdo shooting, 11 January 2015," via Wikimedia Commons, Creative Commons License, 11 January 2015.

[32]Maryam Namazie, "Fear of Offending Muslims Should Not Stop Us Fighting Islamism," *New Statesman,* 19 December 2011.

[33]Charles Walton, *Policing Public Opinion in the French Revolution: The Culture of Calumny and the Problem of Free Speech,* New York: Oxford University Press, 2009.

[34]Photo credit: Tangopaso, "Building at 26 rue Serpollet, Paris 20th arrond," via Wikimedia Commons, Creative Commons License, 11

October 2012.

[35]Kohn, Sally, "Free speech comes with responsibilities," CNN, 11 January 2015.

[36]Photo available on Shutterstock at this address: http://www.shutterstock.com/pic-243316759/stock-photo-strasbourg-france-jan-people-hold-placards-reading-i-am-free-during-a-unity-rally.html?src=UPYlu-Fm3_lxMczSMv77OQ-3-54

[37]Photo credit: Tjebbe van Tijen, "'NOUS SOMMES TOUS CE FLIC' do not let the radicalism of Charlie Hebdo be commodified," 8 January 2015, via Flickr, Creative Commons Attribution.

[38]Photo Credit: Creative Commons Attribution License.

[39]Jack Sommers, "Murdered Police Officer Ahmed Merabet's Brother Malek Says Charlie Hebdo Terrorists 'Pretend To Be Muslims,'" *The Huffington Post UK*, 11 January 2015.

[40]Photo credit: Greenatfifteen, "Islamic Protest in Hyde Park, Sydney 01," via Wikimedia Commons, Creative Commons License CC BY-SA 3.0, 20 September 2012.

[41]Bleich, *The Freedom to Be Racist?*

[42] Roger Cohen, "A 21st-Century Islam," *International Herald Tribune*, 22 September 2012.

[43] Muck, Terry, "Muhammad's Message Rests on Five Pillars." *National Catholic Reporter*, 5 Oct. 2001.

[44] *Law in the Middle East,* Vol. 1: Origin and Development of Islamic Law, eds. Majid Khadduri and Herbert J. Lienbesny, Washington, DC: Middle East Initiative, 1955.

[45]Photo Credit: National Information and Communication Agency, Republic of Indonesia, "Abdurrahman Wahid, fourth President of

Indonesia," Public Domain, via Wikimedia Commons, 2001.

[46]Kyai Haji Abdurrahman Wahid, Preface to Paul Marshall and Nina Shay, *Silenced: How Apostasy and Blasphemy Codes Are Choking Freedom Worldwide*, New York: Oxford University Press, 2011.

[47] Wahid, Preface to *Silenced*.

[48]*The Columbia Encyclopedia*, 6th ed., New York: Columbia University Press, 2014.

[49]"Salman Rushdie Says 'I Stand With Charlie Hebdo' After Paris Attack," *Time,* 7 January 2015.

[50] Wahid, Preface *Silenced*.

[51]Kai Hafez, "Transcultural Communication and the Antinomy between Freedom and Religion: A Comparison of Media Responses to the Rushdie Affair in Germany and the Middle East," *Religion, Law, and Freedom: A Global Perspective*, eds. Joel Thierstein and Yahya R. Kamalipour, Westport, CT: Praeger, 2000.

[52]Wahid, Preface to *Silenced*.

[53] Photo credit: LPLT, "Paris' Grand Mosque," via Wikimedia Commons, Creative Commons License, 1 May 2009.

[54]Paul Marshall and Nina Shea, *Silenced: How Apostasy and Blasphemy Codes Are Choking Freedom Worldwide*, New York: Oxford University Press, 2011.

[55]Catherine Raissiguier, *Reinventing the Republic: Gender, Migration, and Citizenship in France.*, Stanford, CA: Stanford University Press, 2010.

[56]Marshall and Shea, *Silenced*.

[57]Bleich, *The Freedom to Be Racist?*

[58] Bleich, *The Freedom to Be Racist?*

[59]Martin and Shea, *Silenced.*

[60]Martin and Shea, *Silenced.*

[61]Martin and Shea, *Silenced.*

[62]Martin and Shea, *Silenced.*

[63]Bleich, *The Freedom to Be Racist?*

[64]Bleich, *The Freedom to Be Racist?*

[65]Martin and Shea, *Silenced.*

[66]Bleich, *The Freedom to Be Racist?*

[67]Photo Credit: Oliver, "Je suis Charlie," 10 January 2015, via Flickr, Creative Commons Attribution.

[68]Jennifer MacMillan, "Cartoonist Draws Powerful Tribute to Slain Charlie Hebdo Staff," *The Huffington Post* Canada, 7 January 2015.

[69]Abby Phillip and Abby Ohlheiser, "What is Charlie Hebdo, the provocative satirical newspaper attacked by gunmen in Paris?," *Washington Post*, 7 January 2015.

[70]Photo Credit: Valentina Calà, "Je_suis_Charlie-7," 7 January 2015, via Flickr, Creative Commons Attribution.

[71]Robert Hardman, "Night That the Lights Went out on Eiffel Tower," *Daily Mail* (London), 9 January 2015.

[72]Photo Credit: Dominic Alves, "Je suis Charlie," "Graffiti created on the wall of the former Blind Tiger Club on the corner of Grand Parade and Kingswood Street - in Brighton, England, UK - during January 2015," 8 January 2015, via Flickr, Creative Commons Attribution.

[73]Photo Credit: SirPecanGum, "Je suis CHARLIE," 8 January

2015, via Flickr, Creative Commons Attribution.

[74]Photo Credit: erd Casper, "je suis charlie," 12 January 2015, via Flickr, Creative Commons Attribution.

[75]Photo Credit: Chefzwerg, "Je suis CHARLIE," 12 January 2015, via Flickr, Creative Commons Attribution.

[76]David Goldman and Jose Pagliery, "#JeSuisCharlie becomes one of most popular hashtags in Twitter's history," CNN, 9 January 2015.

[77]Brian Reede, "Turn to Twitter and Defeat the Terrorists," *The Mirror* (London, England), 10 January 2015.

[78]Photo Credit: "2014 Pastoral Visit of Pope Francis to Korea," 7 August 2014, Korean Culture and Information Service (Jeon Han), via Wikimedia Commons, Creative Commons License CC BY-SA 2.0.

[79]"Paris attacks: Charlie Hebdo cartoonists' funerals held," BBC News, 15 January 2015.

[80]Philip Pullella, "Pope Francis on Charlie Hebdo attack: 'You can't make fun of faith,'" *The Globe and Mail*, 15 January 2015.

[81]"Salman Rushdie, threatened over book, defends free speech," *New Jersey Herald*, 15 January 2015.

[82]"Financial backers rally to Charlie Hebdo's cause," *enca*, 11 January 2015.

[83]The campaign, "Soutenez Charlie Hebdo et les familles des victimes de l'attentat," was organized by David Opolon and hosted by leetchi.com.

[84]"Charlie Hebdo to print 1 million copies next week," *New York Post*, 8 January 2015.

[85]Sam Schechner, "Charlie Hebdo's New Issue Flies Off

Newsstands," *Wall Street Journal* 14 January 2015.

[86]Sarah Begley and Olivier Laurent, "Where to Buy the New Charlie Hebdo," *Time*, 13 January 2015.

[87]"Buyers of Sold-Out Charlie Hebdo Show Off Cover on Social Media," *Time* 14 January 2015.

[88]L. V. Anderson, "What Does the New Charlie Hebdo Cover Mean? Its Cartoonist Explains," *Slate*, 13 January 2015.

[89]Anderson, "What Does the New Charlie Hebdo Cover Mean?"

[90]"Read the New Issue."

[91]"Read the New Issue."

[92]"Defiant Charlie Hebdo satirizes Muhammad and critiques the Catholic Church," *Crux*, 13 January 2015.

[93]"Read the New Issue."

[94]Simon Tomlinson, "#noapology: Muslims stage angry protests over Charlie Hebdo's Mohammed cartoon as Boko Haram terror leader hails Paris massacre," *Daily Mail*, 14 January 2015.

[95]Italics added. "Read the New Issue."

[96]Maryam Namazie, "Fear of Offending Muslims Should Not Stop Us Fighting Islamism," *New Statesman*, 19 December 2011.

[97]"Read the New Issue."

CPSIA information can be obtained
at www.ICGtesting.com
Printed in the USA
LVHW020736030121
675538LV00016BA/2467